D0065794

What the Spirit Is Saying to the Churches

WHAT THE *S*PIRIT IS SAYING TO THE CHURCHES

LifeChange Books

HENRY BLACKABY

Multnomah® Publishers *Sisters, Oregon*

WHAT THE SPIRIT IS SAYING TO THE CHURCHES
published by Multnomah Publishers, Inc.
© 2003 by Henry T. Blackaby
International Standard Book Number: 1-59052-036-X

Cover image by Getty Images / Will and Deni McIntyre

Unless otherwise indicated, Scripture quotations are from:
The Holy Bible, New King James Version (NKJV)
© 1984 by Thomas Nelson, Inc.
Italics in Scripture quotations are the author's emphasis.
Multnomah is a trademark of Multnomah Publishers, Inc.,
and is registered in the U.S. Patent and Trademark Office.
The colophon is a trademark of Multnomah Publishers, Inc.

Printed in the United States of America

For information:
MULTNOMAH PUBLISHERS, INC. • P.O. BOX 1720 • SISTERS, OR 97759

Library of Congress Cataloging-in-Publication Data

Blackaby, Henry T., 1935-
    What the Spirit is saying to the churches / by Henry Blackaby.
        p. cm.
    ISBN 1-59052-036-X
    1. Church growth—Saskatchewan—Saskatoon. 2. Missions—Saskatchewan. 3.
God—Will. 4. Baptists—Saskatchewan. 5. Saskatoon (Sask.)—Church history. I. Title.

BR575.S27B57 2003
286'.1712425—dc21

                                    2002156087

03 04 05 06 07 08—10 9 8 7 6 5 4 3 2 1 0

To the many dedicated pastors and spiritual leaders

who long to experience God's fullness

in their lives and ministries.

Table of Contents

About the Author

Henry Blackaby was pastor of Faith Baptist Church in Saskatoon, Saskatchewan, Canada, from 1970–82, after serving two churches in California. He went on to hold denominational responsibilities in Vancouver, British Columbia, Canada, and in Atlanta, Georgia, until his retirement in 2000. He is now president of Henry Blackaby Ministries. Henry and his wife, Marilynn, live in Atlanta. They have five children, all in ministry, and thirteen grand-children.

Acknowledgments

I express my deepest gratitude to the faithful and loving people who made up the fellowship of Faith Baptist Church in Saskatoon, Saskatchewan, Canada, during my twelve-year pastorate there, and to the many precious people who became part of the mission churches and the work that unfolded. Much of the labor was done by the laypeople, by pastors of the missions, and through student work at the Theological College. God will give full reward to them.

To my wife, Marilynn, I owe the deepest gratitude. In those years she carried the heaviest of the load at times, spending much time alone while raising our five children.

And to my children I owe a debt too large to pay for their openness to God in their lives and in our family. It was God who called us to be instruments of His activity in our world, and each of our children responded uniquely, making God's assignment more rich and meaningful.

Also, to the hundreds of people who have heard my testimony of God's grace and who have encouraged me over the years to put it in writing, I say, "Thank you."

Finally, Bill Shadle, former minister of music at First Baptist Church, Denton, Texas, who brought his youth choir year after year. He helped to begin and build many of our mission churches. The debt to him, and Maxine his wife, and to his church, is immeasurable. To Lynda McLeod, a Mission Service Corps volunteer and my former secretary, I express my deepest appreciation for her many hours of typing, which made this manuscript possible.

WHEN GOD WORKS

Jesus answered them,
"My Father has been working until now,
and I have been working."
JOHN 5:17

When God does His mighty work in the midst of His people in a particular place, it's overwhelming to those who are there to experience Him. Though it often brings much hard work for them, His presence makes everything worthwhile.

Such an experience also brings a desire by those involved to humbly tell other Christians about the wonderful works of God, though it's too much to be fully and adequately communicated. They share the psalmist's excitement:

The works of the LORD are great,
    Studied by all who have pleasure in them....
He has made His wonderful works to be
    remembered.

PSALM 111:2–4

This book is an account of what happened when the people of one church heard what the Spirit was saying to them and obeyed. They saw God accomplish things that could be explained only in terms of His divine presence and activity.

I was part of that experience, and many have urged me to share these things with others. As I have done so, some respond with skepticism and doubt, often because they've never experienced His work in their lives and do not completely understand it. Still others seem to determine that such things are irrelevant and continue to pursue the world's principles, never knowing what God could have done through them.

But for many others in many churches, the story has helped them come into a new relationship with God and new experiences of His power at work. With excitement they give themselves more fully to God, so that through them He can accomplish even greater things than those described on these pages.

May this account be a witness unto the Lord and an encouragement to you and your church to hear what the Spirit is saying. May you respond in faith and obedience...and experience His presence working through you in revival.

And to Him be the glory.

Henry T. Blackaby

GOD SPEAKS
TO HIS PEOPLE

Thus says the LORD *of hosts:*
"Return to Me," says the LORD *of hosts,*
"and I will return to you,"
says the LORD *of hosts.*
ZECHARIAH 1:3

I have been privileged to visit Christians worldwide. As I
do, I'm usually asked to be a Bible teacher. I share with
them the great truths of God's Word using practical illus-
trations from my own life and ministry. God's people
always respond with a hunger for His reality in their lives
and in their churches.

In fact, the question most often asked of me across the
Christian community is this: "How can Christ become

more real and personal to me?" The next most common question is, "How can I clearly know God's will for my life and my church?"

We must help one another with these concerns. In addition to strengthening our individual walk with God, we must attain a fresh and renewed understanding of how God carries out His will in our world.

God's primary means for achieving His will is the local church, which is a living body of Christ. And the churches that are being mightily used of Him are the ones that have learned to "hear" God.

It is time in all our churches for God's people to experience the real presence of our living Lord guiding us collectively, and to adjust our lives to His purpose and activity. Many believe (and I'm one of them) that we may be the generation of those who are alive on earth when Jesus returns. Therefore, we may indeed be a most significant generation. If we are looking for Christ's return, we of all people must be alert and responsive to all He is doing around us. I have lived with this sensitivity all of my life; I'm now more alert to God than I have ever been, and this

> *It is time to experience the real presence of our living Lord guiding us collectively*

biblical awareness governs my messages to God's people.

God is at work around us, and to accomplish this work He personally communicates His will to His people, inviting each church to join in His activity in specific ways. It is not for us to dream our own dreams of what we want to do for God. This is never the pattern in the Scriptures. God already knows what He is purposing to do through those He calls to Himself. And He's waiting for us to adjust our lives to His purposes so He can work powerfully through us to redeem our lost world.

When we hear His call and respond appropriately, there will be no limit to what God can and will do through His people. But if we do not even recognize when He is speaking, we are in trouble at the very heart of our relationship to Him.

This is true at all levels of our walk with God and with each other. If we in our churches cannot sense what God is telling us, then in moments of crucial decisions we'll continue to have only the opinions of men, not the mind of Christ, to direct us. Our entire mission will be in peril.

THE SPIRIT SPEAKS

God is present in the midst of our churches, just as He was present among the seven churches mentioned in Revelation 2–3, where we find this repeated command to each congregation: "He who has an ear, let him hear what the Spirit says to the churches."

The Spirit is indeed continuing to speak to the churches! He has always revealed His purposes to those He would use, and He does so still today. He will tell us, just as He told those first-century Christians, all about our church's strengths, our specific need for adjustment to Him, and what He intends to accomplish through us. We, too, will hear God's voice saying that He is present among us, that He alone knows what He wants to do through us, and that He alone is to be followed.

Just as those churches in Revelation that heard and responded and were used of God to transform their world in a great revival, so also will it be in our time.

How desperate is the need in our world for churches that hear and follow what the Spirit is telling them! The world in our day wants to see God at work through His people, but unless we hear and obey in the things He assigns us (things that only God can accomplish), the world will not experience Him; they will see only "religion" and be turned away.

This is true also on the personal level. As individuals we must learn

How desperate is the need for churches that hear and follow what the Spirit is telling them!

how to hear God's voice. Without such personal fellowship with God, we'll be practicing mere "religion" rather than living in a relationship with our risen Lord.

"RETURN TO ME"

The churches of our day seem to be at a crossroads. Many appear somewhat afraid to release their lives and their people to God. But others truly desire God's presence and activity and are praying for a great touch from God.

They are discovering that this requires repentance. These believers are being deeply moved by the Spirit of God to return to Him with all their hearts. They hear Him say, "Return to Me, and I will return to you" (Malachi 3:7); "Draw near to God and He will draw near to you" (James 4:8); "The LORD is with you while you are with Him" (2 Chronicles 15:2).

Hear carefully and thoughtfully the heart of God! It is always a cause for trembling to think that our sovereign God, who is holy and just, would ever "plead" this way with His people when they have deliberately departed and strayed from Him.

Jesus issued this same plea from the heart of the Father as He began His ministry: "Repent, for the kingdom of heaven is at hand" (Matthew 4:17). At the end of the New Testament, we hear the same call in the Lord's words to the churches in Revelation; to four of these seven churches He had to say, "Repent" (Revelation 2:5; 2:16; 3:3; 3:19). He has continued to issue this solemn invitation throughout history and to this very hour.

A repenting church is God's condition for revival, and it is always corporate repentance!

God has always desired to work through His people, but they have not always recognized His initiative in their lives or His activity around them. But for those churches who repent—those who take time to hear the Spirit; to believe what He tells them; to adjust their plans, structures, and programs to Him; and then to follow the Lord regardless of how impossible it may seem—these are the churches that will be spiritually renewed and that will experience God's mighty deeds through them to bring a lost world to Himself in a great spiritual awakening.

Chapter 1

GOD TAKES THE INITIATIVE

*"You did not choose Me, but I chose you
and appointed you that you should go and bear fruit,
and that your fruit should remain."*
JOHN 15:16

On a cold Saturday morning—April 4, 1970—my family and I arrived in the city of Saskatoon in Saskatchewan, Canada, where God had called me to pastor a tiny band of His people.

By most outward appearances, Faith Baptist Church was dying. It had been without a pastor for a number of years and had dwindled to only a handful of people. For months a For Sale sign had stood on the front lawn outside their small, white wood-frame building that was several blocks from any major street. Inside the building was a tiled-floor sanctuary where, on Sunday mornings, the walls echoed with the scooting noise of a few metal folding chairs. Mostly empty Sunday school classrooms were below, in a basement prone to frequent flooding. And in the month previous, total giving to the church amounted to only ninety dollars.

But we were sure this was a strategic congregation. A cross-denominational mission study group, Outreach Canada, had indicated that Canada desperately needed 10,000 more church plants immediately just to keep up with population growth. Our denomination (the Southern Baptists) believed that we must do our part—while praying that God would use others as well—and we knew we had our own unique assignment from God. Faith Baptist was our only church in Saskatoon, a city of 135,000 people. In all of Saskatchewan—a province of 950,000—we had as yet only one other church, a mission to North American Natives more than ninety miles away. And in all of Canada, we had no work or presence among two-thirds of the country's 24 million people. We therefore saw Faith Baptist in Saskatoon as a church on the cutting edge, an assembly with a great responsibility for expanding ministry throughout Canada.

For the remnant of people at Faith Baptist, however, thoughts about the future must have seemed about as exciting as the drooping overhang that kept the church's front door from fully opening. The horizon before them indicated little if any evidence of great expansion.

A few months earlier, the ten people who had been hanging on, trying to keep this church alive, had called a meeting to consider disbanding. It seemed impossible that they would ever be able to secure a pastor. As they went to their knees in prayer in that meeting, they thought God wanted them to close the church's doors. But while kneeling, God touched their hearts. They got up saying, "God wants us to try one more time."

They got up saying, "God wants us to try one more time."

And with the possibility of my coming to serve them— I was ministering in a church in Southern California at the time—they told themselves, "If Henry will come to be our pastor, we'll know God isn't through with us yet!" And God wasn't.

PREPARED BY GOD

That cold Saturday morning when we arrived in Saskatoon was a moment God had long ago prepared me for. I grew up in the small city of Prince Regent, British Columbia, on Western Canada's north coast. I had heard the heart cry of my father and mother as they longed and prayed for an evangelical church in our community. During World War II, my father, a businessman, started a church in a dance hall. He preached, my mother played the piano, my older brother ushered, and my younger brother and I were the congregation. It was eight months before we had our first adult visitor. We continued faithfully and experienced slow growth. With much prayer, we were able to see a pastor come to lead us after eight years.

Suddenly, we were faced with an enormous and immediate spiritual challenge.

During those growing-up years, I also became aware of many other towns and villages that had no evangelical witness and often had never had a church. This left a deep impression on my heart that was continuing to shape my life as I responded to God's call and returned to Canada.

But the Blackabys weren't the only new faces to show up at Faith Baptist on that April Saturday in Saskatoon. On the same morning, a car with five men pulled up to join us for lunch. They had come from Prince Albert, a city of thirty thousand people ninety miles to the north. These men had been meeting regularly for Bible study for almost four years and had become convinced God wanted to use them to help start a church in their community. Not only that, but God had laid on their hearts a burden for the numerous other towns, villages, and North American Native reserves in our region that had little or no gospel witness. From their study of the Scriptures, they could foresee God establishing many churches in these places, filled with people of one heart and one mind and one soul, people who would release their lives to Him for the reaching of the unreached.

When these men heard I was coming to Saskatoon, they began to pray. They became convinced God wanted me to be their pastor too, driving up to Prince Albert twice a week. And they had come down to Saskatoon that morning to share with us this "word from the Lord."

Suddenly, Faith Baptist Church was faced with an enormous and immediate spiritual challenge.

A MAJOR DECISION

As a church, we had to decide if this was God's way of speaking to us. It was clear that the yearning in the hearts of God's people in Prince Albert was due to the activity of God. He had clearly led these men to come to us for help. These were things only God could do. Did this mean God was showing us a ministry He wanted us to undertake? Were we to start a mission church in Prince Albert?

Was this our "Macedonian call," like Paul's experience in Acts 16:6–10, when he saw the vision of the man in

Macedonia crying out for help? Was our response to be as Paul's was— "Now after he had seen the vision, immediately we sought to go to Macedonia, concluding that the Lord had called us to preach the gospel to them" (16:10)? It appeared that what God had done in the Scriptures was now happening to us!

Another truth was also present. Almost twenty years earlier as a teenager, I had told the Lord, "If You ever call me into the ministry, and if there are people anywhere within driving distance who want a Bible study or a church, I will go." This commitment had grown out of my experience growing up in a remote area of British Columbia and seeing my parents' faithful commitment to ministry there.

My heart had been fashioned by God to do His will. If people asked me to come, I felt I could not say no. So I, too, was now faced with a major decision. Would I keep my vow to God that I made earlier in my life?

God's Pattern

This was a crucial moment for our little church. God was obviously at work among us. But we felt so helpless and alone, so very weak. And we were so small in numbers.

Faith Baptist had never sponsored a mission church, and I had never pastored a church that pursued this means of ministry. We were certainly not bringing to this situation our strengths, our skills, or our expertise and experience in starting mission churches.

Moreover, some of the people at our church said to me, "Henry, have you ever been in a Saskatchewan blizzard?"

When I said no, they replied, "You can't promise those people you will drive up there twice a week."

All I knew to say was, "The God who could still a storm on the Sea of Galilee can still a storm in Saskatchewan."

As their pastor, I knew I had to help open our people's eyes to the ways of God by leading them into His Word. As I did, they began to see that what we were experiencing agreed with the witness of the Scriptures.

God had shown us where He was at work. The very reason He had revealed this to us was because He was inviting us to join Him in His work. We had to decide if we believed Him, if we were willing to adjust our lives to Him, and if we would trust Him to guide and provide for us as we obeyed.

He had revealed this to us because He was inviting us to join Him in His work.

We realized that this was God's pattern in the Scriptures. We saw it most clearly in how Jesus would conform His actions to whatever activity God the Father was revealing to Him. Jesus explained it this way: "For the Father loves the Son, and shows Him all things that He Himself does"; Jesus therefore was doing nothing on His own, but only "what He sees the Father do"; and whatever God the Father was doing, "the Son also does in like manner" (John 5:19–20).

The Father's activity determined the Son's direction and motivation. The Father took the initiative to show the Son what He was doing, and Jesus then joined Him. And so it should also be for us, we believed.

HE IS ABLE...AND HE WILL

During this critical time for Faith Baptist, a simple, clear word came to us from the Lord as we lingered before Him: "Our God whom we serve is able...and He will" (Daniel 3:17). This confident statement would become an anchor to our souls through the continuing unfolding of God's invitation. It would be our motto in all we were to do in the months and years ahead.

God had spoken. With such assurance, we saw God's assignment for us. We knew God had taken the initiative to come to us, and we believed He would continue to reveal day by day what He wanted to accomplish through us.

How new and different such an approach was to the church! It helped us realize that it did not matter what capacities or abilities our small band of believers possessed or what we thought we could do for God. We sensed rather the truth that God had "chosen the weak things of the world…and the base things of the world and the things which are despised…and the things which are not, to bring to nothing the things that are, that no flesh should glory in His presence" (1 Corinthians 1:27–29).

Could we, as such a small church, sponsor a mission church? We sensed that this was the wrong question. The right question was this: Had God revealed His will for us? And if so, would we believe, obey, and trust Him?

We answered by saying yes. God was at work and He was letting us see what He was doing and how He wanted to work through us. We were ready to experience in a new way His presence and power working through us to reach others.

Over time we came to be convinced that God would indeed use us to accomplish His purposes. And I would learn that a church's name can mean so much. The months and years before us would prove that the word Faith truly expressed this people's character. When a church realizes it all depends on God, not them, and will together yield their lives fully to Him, God begins to work. It doesn't depend on numbers, status, skills, or even resources. The future depends on God and on His people who will hear Him, believe Him, and obey Him.

Chapter 2

WHAT ONLY GOD CAN DO

"Where I am, there My servant will be also."
JOHN 12:26

Christians are at a crucial time in human history. Today more than ever, God's people need to hear His voice, then stand afresh before Him—in our personal lives and in our churches—to trust Him to do all He promises.

But how do church members know what God is saying to them? How can they recognize His voice? How can they clearly grasp what God intends to do through them as a church? And what adjustments will be required by His people for God to work mightily again through them?

TRUTH IS A PERSON

To discover these things and live them out, we at Faith Baptist believed we together needed a fresh orientation of our lives to the Lord Jesus. We began a year's study—on Sunday mornings, Sunday evenings, and Wednesday nights—of the life of Christ as portrayed in the Gospels. Jesus had taken twelve men, and for three and a half years He had taught them and oriented them to Himself and to God's kingdom. We studied this together and helped one another understand what it meant for us.

We remembered how Jesus had said (in John 17:3) that eternal life means fully experiencing Him and the Father. We realized that to follow Him we must know Him in this way—in our minds, in our hearts, and in our lives—to the degree that we could sense how and where He wanted us to follow.

Knowing Truth in this relational way would set our church free.

We soon sensed deeply that truth was more than just a concept or principle; rather, Truth was a person (as Jesus said in John 14:6— "I am…the truth") who was present in and among us as the head of our church. Practically speaking, this meant that we should never evaluate any situation simply by what we ourselves saw, heard, or felt. Rather, we were to hear from

Him regarding the situation—and only then could we know the truth about it.

For example, in our study we looked at the time when the disciples were suddenly caught in a storm at sea. If we had been able to ask them in that moment, "What is the truth of this situation?" they would have replied, "We are perishing." Was that true? It might well have been, had not Jesus been present. But Truth was asleep in the back of their boat. Only when He stood up and calmed the storm and the sea did they know the truth of their situation.

We saw that knowing Truth in this relational way would set our church free, a freedom that would come only from hearing and abiding in the Lord's Word, just as He said: "If you abide in My word, you are My disciples indeed. And you shall know the truth, and the truth shall make you free" (John 8:31–32). As we studied the Bible, we realized we were standing before Him, hearing His Word. We were receiving Him fully as He revealed Himself and His ways to us in the Scriptures.

FACE-TO-FACE WITH GOD

Jesus had said, "I am the way, the truth, and the life" (John 14:6). For three and a half years with His disciples, Jesus had filled those words with meaning. Wherever He was, all the life of God was both present and active! The blind received their sight, the deaf could hear, lepers were healed, the dead were raised, storms were stilled, and multitudes were fed. Jesus was their life! He was the "I AM" of the New Testament.

We suddenly found ourselves face-to-face with God.

In the Old Testament, God the Father had been "I AM" to His people as He brought them out of Egypt with a mighty hand. He assured Moses and the children of Israel that He Himself was everything they required. They encountered situations they had never before experienced and had no visible means of sustenance for their journey, but at every point of their need, as they obeyed God's direction, He was their life. He was present to meet every situation.

Now we, too, were hearing His Word, not only personally, but also corporately as a church. In familiar passages like these, we suddenly found ourselves face-to-face with God:

> He who has begun a good work in you will complete it until the day of Jesus Christ.
> PHILIPPIANS 1:6

> I can do all things through Christ who strengthens me.
> PHILIPPIANS 4:13

My God shall supply all your need according to
His riches in glory by Christ Jesus.
PHILIPPIANS 4:19

"Call to Me, and I will answer you, and show you
great and mighty things, which you do not know."
JEREMIAH 33:3

In Him dwells all the fullness of the Godhead
bodily; and you are complete in Him.
COLOSSIANS 2:9–10

In all these things we are more than conquerors
through Him who loved us.
ROMANS 8:37

We became convinced that all these Scriptures were
true for us, as the Holy Spirit made them real. In each one,
God was revealing Himself to us. We began to experience
Him. His life became our life.

Week after week I taught God's people the truth of
how God would keep revealing more about Himself and
His activity as we came to Him and continued responding to His presence. I illustrated this from Scripture as
well as pointing out whatever "activity of God" He was
showing us in and around our own lives. When we
clearly saw what God was doing, we knew we were to

respond to Him and join in His activity. We could proceed with confidence, knowing His presence would make the difference.

For example in Romans 3:10–12, Paul reminds us that because of the effects of sin none of us on our own is righteous or understands God's ways or seeks after God; each of us has turned away to a life that is empty and vain. This means that God Himself must work within us (1) to cause us to seek after Him (as Jesus teaches us in John 6:44–45 and 6:65), and (2) to enable us to understand God and His truth and His ways. For all these things the active work of the Holy Spirit is required (John 14:26; 16:13–14; 1 Corinthians 2:9–16).

Therefore we learned to look for people who were seeking after God, being drawn to Christ, and inquiring after spiritual things. These were things only God could bring about; when we saw Him doing them, we were to recognize and respond to Him.

These truths became a real and practical guide for us. To see God at work became a way of life. There were things only God could do, and when He revealed these to us and we saw them happening, we acknowledged it and responded to Him as best we knew, adjusting our lives to Him. God then responded by opening to us more of His will.

How Practical!

Often, when I talk to others about God's being present and active and involved practically like this in our work, someone will tell me I sound like a "mystic," like someone who isn't practical. Meanwhile, the self-described "practical" person seems to be pursuing ministry by his own effort and means, then asking God to bless it.

Was God's presence practical in the parting of the Red Sea? Was His presence practical for the children of Israel in providing them with manna and water, in defeating the Amalekites, and in guiding them with a pillar of cloud by day and a pillar of fire by night?

Was God's presence in Jesus Christ practical in restoring sight to a blind man, in healing a leper, in stilling a storm, and in feeding the multitudes?

Was the presence of God's Spirit practical on the day of Pentecost and in releasing Peter from prison and in guiding Paul when he was shipwrecked?

Is the presence of the living Christ practical as head over our churches in supplying our needs and giving us victories?

Is God's presence practical? The answer, of course, is yes. But we as a church were constantly faced with this key question: From what we learned in the Scriptures, could we practice God's presence in the carrying out of His will?

Would God really make a practical difference—or was everything (or at least almost everything) up to us?

In expressing one of the many paradoxes of the kingdom, Paul said, "His grace toward me was not in vain; but I labored more abundantly than they all, yet not I, but the grace of God which was with me" (1 Corinthians 15:10).

Our labor was to be all of God and His grace; yet, because it was, we were to labor more than all others, remembering it was not our labors, but it would be both. God would work mightily with and through us as we labored to do His will—even when we saw no possible human means to accomplish it. God's grace would sustain us.

We knew it would have to be that way, because if we were to rely on our own strengths, we could not accomplish much; we were too few in number, our resources were too limited, and we knew of no one else who would help us. We were entirely dependent on God.

SERVANTS TO THE MASTER

As we continued our study of Christ's ministry, we understood that we were the Lord's servants and that as servants we were to look to the Master—as head of the church—to lead us, rather than taking the initiative and deciding on our own what to do. As Lord, He alone had the right to initiate activity and give direction. Jesus said, "Where I am, there My servant will be also" (John 12:26). We knew He was at work, and as His servants we were to follow closely enough to recognize what He was doing, then adjust our lives and our church to Him so He could complete His work through us.

This did not mean inactivity or just sitting back and waiting. We were to be always looking for Him and ready to join Him; and when we did join in, we had to work hard to keep up with God's plans, knowing it was His grace that accomplishes all as He worked in and through us.

The story of Faith Baptist Church would become the story of the living Christ expressing His presence in and through us. We were strengthened in our faith and prepared for greater and greater things. Abundant joy would replace the despair that had for several years immobilized God's people in our church.

With Jesus' presence in our lives and church, we would never be the same again.

Chapter 3

SEEING GOD WORK

Therefore, my beloved, as you have always obeyed...
work out your own salvation with fear and trembling;
for it is God who works in you [as a church]
both to will and to do for His good pleasure.
PHILIPPIANS 2:12–13

God's people at Faith Baptist had obeyed His invitation to sponsor a mission church in Prince Albert, and for two years I continued making the twice-a-week drive northward from Saskatoon. Not once did a storm prevent me from taking God's Word to His children in Prince Albert.

One of my first visits there was for a Bible study and prayer meeting held in a farmhouse beside a cattle feedlot. Twelve people were present. I wondered why God had brought me from the midst of 7.5 million people in the Los Angeles area to such a place as this in northern Saskatchewan.

After the Bible study, we knelt to pray. The woman next to me began to weep as she thanked the Lord for hearing their prayers of many years for Him to send a pastor to teach them God's Word. I wept also and thanked God for inviting me to join Him in what He was doing and what He was going to do through His people there. I was God's answer to their prayers.

Those two years of going to Prince Albert to minister were full of challenges. On one trip during particularly cold weather, I traveled with a heavy heart. Marilynn's health had taken a bad turn after the birth of our fifth child, a little girl, and she was emotionally exhausted.

When I arrived that cold day in Prince Albert, no one showed up. My heart sank. Briefly I wondered if I should continue our outreach there. God assured me I was to be obedient and that He would build his church in Prince Albert and the surrounding region.

God had revealed earlier to us His activity in Prince Albert, and we had immediately obeyed His invitation. As best we could, we had been faithful to our call, and from this beginning, God would reveal His larger purpose.

THE COSTS OF FAITHFULNESS

Continuing this ministry meant that for two years I was gone from Sunday dinners with my family, our car wore out much quicker, and Marilynn and our five children were frequently alone. One day, as I prepared to leave for the drive north, Marilynn began to cry and told me, "I can't take it anymore." We stood in the living room and cried. We also cried out to God. We were doing together what He had directed us to do, but the strain was almost too much.

As we prayed, God seemed to become so real and personal, flooding us with peace and assurance. Marilynn felt His presence and told me, "I know you must go. They don't have the gospel. I'll be all right; God has given me assurance and peace. I just needed you for a little while."

The Lord did sustain us and freed us to continue His work. In our obedience—day after day, month after month—we experienced His activity, confirming what we believed to be His Word to us.

We also became convinced that a church must expect the Lord's assignment to be something only God can do. He would accomplish what was impossible for us on our own so He could reveal Himself to His people and to our world through His people. All His children would know that He alone had done it, and they would worship Him and trust Him in their lives and churches.

> *A church must expect the Lord's assignment to be something only God can do.*

These truths represented a radical change of thinking in our church in Saskatoon. Everything about this venture was so new, and we saw how many adjustments were required to enable us to be God's instruments. We also realized deeply that there's a real cost in doing the will of God, both for an individual and for a church.

For me, I began to see that my greatest point of hesitation in obeying this calling from God was not what it would cost me, but what it would cost my family and church. God caused me to remember that Jesus' obedience to do the Father's will on the cross was like an arrow through the heart of His mother; and as for the disciples, the Lord's obedience would eventually bring them to the place of martyrdom. Christ's obedience was costly not only to Himself, but also to those around Him.

For Faith Baptist, the cost included picking up the ministry load in Saskatoon in my absence, sharing resources with our brothers and sisters in Prince Albert (and later in other locations), and eventually mortgaging Faith Baptist's building and property to secure a facility for the believers in Prince Albert.

The costs were real—but we gained so much more by seeing new believers come to know the Lord in Prince Albert and later become so vital to our further expanding work.

More Responsibilities

In time, the believers in Prince Albert not only obtained property and a church building and called a pastor of their own, but in turn launched several other mission churches—in Love, Melfort, Tisdale, Leoville, and Smeaton—as well as Bible studies and ministries in many other communities, plus several significant ministries to North American Natives in a number of locations.

We soon realized the truth of the Lord's words when He told His disciples that if they were faithful in a little, He would give them even more responsibilities (Matthew 25:21; Luke 16:10). To God's people at Faith Baptist, the Lord began entrusting other communities—including Regina, Blaine Lake, Lanigan, Wynyard, Allan, LeRoy, and Kyle—who called on us to "come over and help." Whenever people in a town or village indicated their deep and prolonged praying for a church (some had been praying for decades), we felt this was God's invitation to join Him, and we began a Bible study in that community that we knew would lead to a church.

We didn't need to take a survey to see how many prospects there were in that location. Wherever God indicated He was working, we were obedient to follow, again remembering His words: "Where I am, there My servant will be also." In responding this way, we had as many as ten mission churches going at once, despite our church's small size.

The story of our being led to minister in the town of Kyle is representative of how we recognized God's activity and joined in. One day when a college student was baptized in our church, a friend of hers who was in attendance began weeping. Later I spoke with this young woman, and the Lord used me to deepen her faith.

Then she told me that people in her community had been praying for twenty-three years for someone to begin a church there. She was from Kyle, a town sixty-five miles southwest of Saskatoon. "Could you come and meet with us?" she asked.

Our full church was told about the woman's invitation. We knew this had to be a work of God, and a few of us traveled to Kyle, praying that we would recognize whatever God would have us see and experience.

They told us of their praying with tears, and they begged us to return regularly.

In Kyle, nineteen adults were gathered. They told us of their praying with tears and they begged us to return regularly. We carefully reported this to the others at Faith Baptist and looked again at Scripture. We became convinced that God was inviting us to join His work there in Kyle. We accepted His invitation, and God established another of His churches.

Interestingly, the first adult convert there was the "town drunk"; he became a good witness whose testimony affected not only Kyle, but other towns as well.

What happened in the town Allan is another example. We were led to hold a Vacation Bible School one summer there while we looked to see what else God would reveal to us of His activity there. On the final day of this outreach, a woman came forward to us and said, "I've been praying for thirty years for an evangelical church for Allan." God was letting us know where He was working. We were convinced this was His way of inviting us to join Him in this work and begin a church there. Today there is a thriving church in Allan, and through them a mission church in Watrous and Bible studies in Young and other nearby communities.

As God took the initiative to reveal His activity to us, we responded. And when we did, He accomplished His greater purposes through us.

WHAT GOD BEGAN

As the Holy Spirit worked in and through us in ever-expanding activity, we pioneered ministries in larger cities (in Saskatchewan's capital, Regina, plus another work in Saskatoon, and several missions in Winnipeg, Manitoba) as well as in the smaller communities. Many of our people were called into ministry and trained, and multitudes were saved and added to God's people.

God did everything—and so much more than we could ask or think—according to His power that worked in our midst (Ephesians 3:20–21). We discovered that He was sufficient to meet every need we encountered. He provided the leaders we asked for, the finances we requested, the wisdom we prayed for, and the peace and comfort we cried out for when we were afraid. In providing all the finances we needed, He was never late and never short (and, as my wife, Marilynn, would often add, never early!). He provided full-time pastors for every church we obediently started.

Over time, as we continued abiding in the Scriptures, the Holy Spirit laid on our hearts the certainty that if we would be faithful to believe Him, "all things are possible to him who believes" (Mark 9:23), and "nothing will be impossible for you" (Matthew 17:20). God assured us that He would use us to establish churches all across our province and all across Canada. Our Lord's commission was "Go into all the world and preach the gospel to every creature" (Mark 16:15). My heart was constantly burdened for all of our nation, and this became increasingly true of the entire

He was never late and never short—and never early!

church. We learned from Scripture to pray for laborers to lead the new works He would begin. We cried to the Lord for leaders, knowing that if Canada was to know the Savior, Canadians would have to participate.

He then kept bringing into our spiritual awareness the University of Saskatchewan, just a few blocks away from our church in Saskatoon. We began to have the assurance that we should faithfully witness on this campus.

God's Word and our response were again put to the test. We had no college students in our church at the time, and neither I nor anyone in the church had ever done student ministry. But as we prayed and listened and shared with one another, God gave us one heart and mind to accept this invitation.

There was an immediate response. A law professor from the University and his daughter came to us and were baptized in our church, and his wife joined as a member as well. They were convinced God was adding them to our little fellowship. The truth of this was soon obvious to us all as this family became the backbone of our developing congregation.

We continued to pray and work. Eleven students from a Baptist Student Union at the University of Washington in the United States called to say they had been praying for months to know God's direction for the coming summer. They told us God had strongly impressed upon them a plan to come to Saskatoon to help us begin a student ministry at the University of Saskatchewan. They asked us, "Do you have a need?"

With joy we told of our prayers for God to show us how to do His will on the campus. The students came in answer to our prayers. One of them, Joe Rust, was burdened to stay for several years and led our church to fulfill this mission assignment from God to the campus. In the next decade, we baptized about 160 students from the University, more than half of whom felt God's call into the ministry or missions. Many are now pastoring churches across Canada or serving the Lord on other mission fields.

Another assignment soon became real to us as well. If God was going to call students into the ministry, they needed to be trained, and many would not be able to attend any of our denomination's seminaries in the United States. After much prayer and clearly sensing God's leadership, our church began the Christian Training Center, later renamed the Canadian Baptist Theological College (and subsequently merged into an entirely new institution, the Canadian Southern Baptist Seminary in Alberta). To our joy and amazement, more than four hundred students attended classes at our training college in the decade that followed. God had heard our cry to Him to send forth His laborers into His harvest field (Matthew 9:37–38)!

LOSING OUR LIVES

We were learning that as we were faithful to whatever God placed in our hands, the outcome would be other assignments. The costs would continue; as God blessed His Word in other places, we as a church would need to deny self to meet others' needs. We would be asked to "lose" our lives; but in return we knew that we would "save" them (Matthew 16:25).

These increased responsibilities and costs brought much heart searching in our families and in our church. In our families and as a church we felt a partnership as well as a pain in our sense of God's direction—we knew that many would be denied the gospel if we kept it to ourselves.

God had begun to show us He had much to do through our church if we were willing to hear Him, believe Him, obey Him, and trust Him to provide for our needs.

Chapter 4

HEARING HIM

"Indeed I have spoken it; I will also bring it to pass.
I have purposed it; I will also do it."
ISAIAH 46:11

The Spirit of God puts the people of God into the presence of God. And in His presence, the Spirit reveals God's purposes to the church He would use. He then waits for our response.

What should that response look like?

We learned at Faith Baptist that we could think of our proper response to the Lord as a church in these terms:

1. Hear Him afresh. God never hides the truth. He is always open and honest with us. We are the ones who tend to overlook, or not hear, all that God is saying. He is always taking the initiative to make His assignment known, and we must be actively alert to receive it.

2. Believe Him wholeheartedly. We must determine that God is everything He says He is and will do everything He says He will do for us—if we let Him. As He calls us to accomplish the impossible, we know He'll provide everything we need, because to be on mission with God through His church is to be in the midst of the most practical and extensive concentration of God's resources possible.

3. Adjust to Him—unconditionally—in our lives and in our churches, in order to join in God's revealed activity. God has the right to require and to make these adjustments in us in order to conform us to Himself and to His will—regardless of how long the process takes.

4. Obey Him—immediately and in faith, as He leads us. He will then accomplish His purposes through us. And His purpose is that every local church become a mission strategy center, reaching out not only to their immediate community, but to the world beyond.

Any church willing to respond this way in their relationship with God will experience His mighty deeds through them to bring a lost world to Himself.

In the remaining pages of this book, let us examine more closely each of these components of our response.

HEARING HIM TOGETHER

It took time as a church for us to search the Scriptures so the Holy Spirit could teach us how we would know when

God was speaking. We needed to be a God-centered and God-saturated church. This required of me as a pastor the same thing it required of Jesus with His disciples: teaching, teaching, teaching!

The Scriptures were our textbook, and I and others were the teachers, though there were clearly times when each of us were teachers and each of us were pupils and learners. As we followed in this pathway, we realized not only how much we needed God, but also how we desperately needed each other.

Just as important as our understanding of God was our coming to know who we were as a church. As we studied the Scriptures, we realized that we were more than just an organization; we were a living body of Christ (1 Corinthians 12:27; Ephesians 1:22–23; 4:16), and each person among us was uniquely united to Christ, the head of our body (1 Corinthians 12).

We knew we were to respect what God was saying through each member.

Each of our members was also uniquely related in a mutual interdependence with one another (Ephesians 4:7, 11–16). And each person was created by God to be on mission with Christ in our world for the Father's redemptive purposes (Mark 16:15–20).

For these reasons, we knew we were to respect what

God was saying through each member. Christ, the head, was actively guiding the body (our church) through each of its members. As He spoke to any member, all of us needed to listen and hear what He was saying through that person to our church.

EVERYONE SHARING

This took constant teaching. In worship services, in personal conversations, in committee meetings and prayer meetings, and even during business meetings, I constantly encouraged each member to study Scripture and to let the Holy Spirit teach them. I then urged them (and often helped them) to share with God's gathered people what He had taught. A constant sense of expectancy developed in the church.

They were given many opportunities, under my guidance as pastor, to let the rest of the body know what God was doing. This was very difficult at first, for they had not been used to doing it. "Canadians are very private people," they reminded me. But soon the sharing began to flow. It happened not only in our times of worship together (usually at the close of a service), but also in our various meetings together and in personal conversations. Many members called the church office and shared what God was saying to them in their devotional times. Others let us know what they experienced at work or at school.

The entire church became more aware of Christ's presence in our midst. He was teaching us how to recognize His activity in our lives together as a church.

We kept growing in our ability to share our lives intimately and purposefully to help each one become more like Christ and to function where God put him in the body. We saw that living together in such a relationship with Christ and one another, we would grow each of us and all of us in spiritual maturity, enabling us to be more responsive to Christ and to experience Him on mission in our world. We knew He would be able to work much more extensively through a mature body than an immature one.

Such a relationship is what I knew the Scriptures meant by koinonia, the word translated "fellowship" in the New Testament (see especially 1 John 1:3–7). Koinonia is a deep bond of love, partnership, and the total sharing of our lives for the well-being of each other, "till we all come to the unity of the faith and of the knowledge of the Son of God, to a perfect man, to the measure of the stature of the fullness of Christ" (Ephesians 4:13). In this bond we grew together.

EVEN IN BUSINESS MEETINGS

Our business meetings became some of our most exciting times in the church's life together. We realized that our corporate decisions were to reflect God's direction and activity in our midst.

As we discussed an issue, we did not ask for a vote—a show of hands for or against a certain course of action (such as whether to start another new mission church). We were not seeking our opinions, but God's will. So we asked instead, "How many sense, after information and prayer, that God is definitely leading us in this direction?"

We did not ask for a vote. We were not seeking our opinions, but God's will.

What happened next, we believed, was God indicating His will to us as a living body. If the consensus was 55 percent positive, we did not immediately proceed with the course of action. Instead, we realized that God was showing us two things: (1) He was moving us in that particular direction, but (2) the timing was not right, since 45 percent had no clear guidance from Him in that direction. So we waited until God brought us all to one heart and mind. We needed to wait on Him until He had adjusted all of us to Himself. God was in charge, and He could bring us all to the "same mind" (Romans 12:16; 15:5–6; 1 Corinthians 1:10). We developed a confident patience in the Lord and a loving trust in each other.

We also realized that what most often caused impatience among us was having to wait for something that only God could do. So we learned to wait on His faithfulness, and we were never disappointed.

GOD BRINGS NEW MEMBERS

In our times of worship together, we began to acknowledge corporately that God alone could save people, and He alone could bring His people to brokenness, dedication, and joy.

We also came to recognize that God alone could add members to our church. He did this as it pleased Him, adding specific members for His purpose in shaping the body to match His assignment (1 Corinthians 12:18). This truth I had to thoroughly teach God's people. In time, with each new member, we became more aware that Christ was active and at work in and through us.

When individuals came for membership, after they confessed before the congregation their repentance and baptism, we also publicly asked each one of them whether they clearly believed God was adding them to our church family. As they answered affirmatively, I would then say publicly to the church: "You have heard their testimony; do you believe God has done a saving work in their lives and is now adding them to our church?"

If they together affirmed this, I then asked the church and the person joining us to publicly commit to opening their lives to one another as God developed us all to Christlikeness and to being faithful to help each other in whatever needs we had. I then asked, "Do we then enter into this solemn covenant relationship to thus honor God's activity among us?"

In this way, God "added to the church daily those who were being saved" (Acts 2:47). We knew that if we as a church gave careful encouragement and care to the new members God called to join us, He would show us how He would train each of them and send them across our nation and around the world.

Chapter 5

BELIEVING HIM

"Then you will know that I am the LORD,
for they shall not be ashamed who wait for Me."
ISAIAH 49:23

In the twelve years I was pastor of Faith Baptist, one of the greatest results in our lives of being on mission with God was the strengthening of our faith.

Knowing that "without faith it is impossible to please Him" (Hebrews 11:6), we did not ask God to give us all we needed ahead of time before we proceeded with a new responsibility He had called us to. All we needed was a word from Him and we stepped forward—trusting God to provide what was lacking. He always did. Increasingly, it never crossed our minds that God would not meet our needs.

This was our experience in building a library and recruiting a faculty for our theological college. It was true when we began a new facility at Faith Baptist when we had less than $2,000 in our building fund, knowing it could cost $220,000. It was true as well when we agreed to buy or build facilities for the churches in Prince Albert, Allan, Kyle, Leroy, Love, and Regina.

It was true when we encouraged our students to apply for seminary training without visible means to support them. It was true when we invited pastors and their families to come and lead mission churches when we had no money to move them or support them.

Not once was God short or late in providing for our needs. But not once did His provision come before we had obediently proceeded to do all we knew to do. As a result, we grew in trust and love toward our Lord, and all who were watching us were encouraged in their own responses to Him.

STRETCHED TO THE LIMIT

With each new mission or ministry we began, we were stretched to the limit in believing Him and trusting Him practically for financial and other needs.

If we were to begin mission churches, who would pastor them? How would we move pastors to the field? How would we support the pastors? All of this would require finances, and at that time there were no funds available for this work through our denomination.

As believers we often sing and say that we love God and trust Him, but when we learn what He is asking or where He is directing, yet we cannot see the practical means needed to accomplish it, too often we mistakenly conclude that God must not be in this after all. At Faith Baptist we knew God's intentions; we knew what ministry paths He was leading us to follow. Now it became painfully clear that our actions would reveal how much we really believed in Him.

Many of our members had never had to "walk by faith" for finances, so we taught them from the Scriptures how God never leads His people where He does not adequately and fully provide. When there were strong questions about this from God's people, we never saw it as "opposition," but rather as a need for more guidance and help in walking by faith. When great faith is required, great patience is required as well. People are more important than projects, so we often waited patiently for those who were weaker in faith; in time they always responded and were grateful for our having loved and cared

> *It became painfully clear that our actions would reveal how much we really believed in Him.*

for them. I taught those who were more mature in their faith to be patient and long-suffering and gentle and kind with the others. That's what love is like (1 Corinthians 13:4), and the fruit of the Spirit brings it to reality in a church (Galatians 5:22).

THRUST FORTH BY GOD

As we went to the Scriptures for God's directions, we saw what our major role was in the securing of laborers for these new ministries. God told us to pray—that was our part. Jesus said, "Pray the Lord of the harvest to send out [or "thrust out"] laborers into His harvest" (Matthew 9:38). The thrusting out of the laborers was God's part.

God told us to pray—that was our part.

But how practical was this? We had always thought we were to go to men and urge them to join us in the harvest field and ask God to bless our efforts. But the Scriptures said we were to pray—then look to see where God was thrusting forth a laborer. When we saw God doing this, we were to join in His activity, agreeing with Him and acting on it.

Our first need for a pastor was in Prince Albert, two years after we began the work there. We prayed, and the first people God laid on our hearts were Jack and Bonna Conner of California. Jack and I had been prayer partners in seminary, and we had kept in touch. We shared our need with Jack and Bonna, and prayed for God to thrust them forth if they were to come. We had no money to move them and no money to support them. But we did need a pastor.

Jack called later to say they not only felt God's strong hand upon them, but had already sold their home to come, regardless of any other factor. No mention was made of salary or other support. We agreed God was indeed thrusting them forth, and we told them to obey God and come, and we would make every effort to help them.

Now the finances. How would we move them from California to Canada? God had said He would provide for our every need as we put His kingdom first (Matthew 6:31–34). We prayed as a church once again. A few days later I received a phone call from First Baptist Church in Fayetteville, Arkansas. The caller said, "Someone told us of your work. We've put all our mission offerings together and have a percentage set aside for Saskatchewan missions. Use it as you will."

The amount they were sending us was $1,500—the exact amount required for the Conners' moving expenses.

This pattern of God's provision was to be repeated again and again over the following years.

TESTED

One day at a conference in Edmonton, Alberta, I talked with another seminary classmate, Len Koster, a Canadian. We discussed the need for churches in the hundreds of towns and villages in Canada with no evangelical witness, including places that had never had a church. I told Len our church was praying for someone to come and help equip us as a church to reach new communities all across Saskatchewan and eventually across the nation.

Len began to weep. He said God had touched his heart; and he would return home and talk with his wife, Ruth, and pray for the mind of God.

Within the week, he called and said, "Henry, God is literally thrusting us forth to come and work with you."

I told him we had no money to move them or to pay them. "But we will pray with you for God's provision. God has never failed us yet, and we're confident He will not fail you either." Len indicated they would pay for the move themselves, if necessary. And they did, moving a thousand miles to work with us as our minister of missions outreach. Then followed one of the most memorable answers to prayer in my life.

When the Kosters had been with us only a short time, Len came to my office to talk. For fourteen years he had been serving as a pastor while also working at a service station to provide their living expenses. "Henry, the need is so great here, I believe God wants me to work full time." He told me he and his wife had been able over the years to save seven thousand dollars, hoping someday to buy their own home. "As we prayed last night," Len said, "God reminded us this money was His and we were to use it to support ourselves until it is gone. God promised us that He would take care of us after that. So don't worry about us."

When he left my office, I fell on my face before God and wept, pouring out my heart to Him. I didn't think this was fair to the Kosters.

I fell on my face before God and wept, pouring out my heart.

Two days later, still upset, I received a letter from a Presbyterian layman I didn't know from Kamloops, British Columbia. The letter read, "I understand a man by the name of Len Koster has come to work with you in starting churches. God told me I am to have a part in his ministry. Enclosed is a check for seven thousand dollars for his support."

Again I fell on my knees, weeping, asking the Lord to forgive me and thanking Him for His love and kindness. When the Kosters and the church learned of God's provision, we were all strengthened in the Lord and were greatly encouraged to continue reaching out in obedience to every town where He would lead us to go.

No pulling on our hearts was any heavier than the securing of salary support for the pastors of our mission churches. Steady, fervent, believing prayer was made for each of them day after day. God always answered with His provision, and it was always adequate. We were learning how to believe the Lord when He said:

> "Therefore do not worry, saying, 'What shall we eat?' or 'What shall we drink?' or 'What shall we wear?...' For your heavenly Father knows that you need all these things. But seek first the kingdom of God and His righteousness, and all these things shall be added to you."
>
> MATTHEW 6:31–33

OUR TURN

God's timely and practical provision was also shown to us when we sought land or buildings for our mission churches. The way these needs were met was so different in each situation that it reinforced our conviction that this wasn't about any method or formula that worked, but about a Person who provided, a Person to follow and trust.

Earlier I mentioned that we mortgaged our church building in Saskatoon to secure a loan to buy a building for the church in Prince Albert. At the time, some of the men in Faith Baptist observed that, though they knew this was what God wanted us to do, it would mean our being unable to get a first mortgage for ourselves when we needed to build.

I replied, "No, it means that when our turn comes to build, the God who is providing now for them will provide for us in our time of need."

Five years later, when we were ready to build our new church building in Saskatoon, that's exactly what God did, in a way that happened only once. I was a guest speaker at a church in Texas. After the service, a man asked to speak with me and said, "Something happened to me tonight as you spoke. I just sold my business, and God told me I am to give you the tithe from this sale."

> *"The God who is providing now for them will provide for us in our time of need."*

His check arrived two weeks later, for $25,000— the amount needed to clear the first mortgage from our church and allow us to get our loan. I reminded our men of our previous conversation and of God's faithfulness.

GOD PROVIDES

Another memorable occasion came in God's provision for our mission church in Allan, forty miles east of Saskatoon. We found a restaurant building for sale on Allan's Main

Street—with a main floor we could use for worship services, a basement for classrooms, and a two-bedroom suite on the second floor that we could use as a parsonage.

The asking price was $15,000. The owner said he would take $9,000 down and carry the remaining $6,000 at 6 percent interest.

We told him we would let him know in two weeks.

At the time we were $100,000 short of our own building needs, so we didn't have nine cents, let alone the $9,000 down payment. As a church we agreed to pray and specifically ask the Father to provide from His riches.

A few days later, a man called from the missions committee of a church in Texas. They had heard about our mission work and were thinking of providing us with $5,000 (plus $200 a month more for a pastor's support). They wanted to know if we had a need for it. I told him what we were praying for God's people in Allan.

A week later a pastor called and said, "We've heard of your mission work. I have a lady whose late husband was an evangelist, and she wants to give $1,000 for a mission work. Do you have a need?" I told him about Allan.

So at the end of two weeks, we had received $6,000—still $3,000 short of the required down payment. We went back to the building's owner in Allan, but before we could say anything, he told us, "By the way, I've been thinking about income tax, and it would be better for me if you gave me $6,000 down and I carried the $9,000 at 6 percent interest."

We answered, "Sir, we were about to propose just that arrangement."

Including God in the Budget

In the middle of our mission assignments, we had another major lesson to learn about finances. In a budget-planning meeting one year, a man observed that I had taught them to walk by faith in every area of our church's life, except that of setting the budget. "When we set our budget," he explained, "it's always on the basis of what we believe we can do. Our budget never reflects that we expect God to do anything."

Painfully, I had to admit he was right.

We decided to set up a budget with these four columns:

1. What we felt we could do (with faith).

2. What others had said they would help us do.

3. What we were going to ask God to do in addition, through prayer.

4. The total, reflecting what we believed it would take to do everything we believed God was asking of us.

Under the old method, our annual budget that year would have been $74,000. With the new approach we set it for $164,000. We presented this enthusiastically to the church, along with the reminder that we would need to be faithful to pray.

As we looked at the report each month in the year that followed, God always gave more than we did. We ended the year with an income of $172,000.

The character of our church was indeed coming to match its name—Faith. Each situation of need created an opportunity for us to trust Him and an opportunity for God to reveal His provision. How kind and personal we found God to be! And we grew to know Him and love Him because of it.

Chapter 6

ADJUSTING TO HIM

> *"And whoever does not bear his cross and come after Me*
> *cannot be My disciple....So likewise, whoever of you*
> *does not forsake all that he has cannot be My disciple."*
> LUKE 14:27, 33

How does a small band of discouraged, disheartened believers become a strong, mature, confident, faith-filled church on mission with their Lord in the world around them?

How does any church get vitally involved with God in this way?

The core answer is this: By adjusting our lives to the presence and activity of our living Lord, one day at a time. As we hear Him and believe Him, and as we see God at work, we make whatever adjustments are necessary in our lives and in our church in order to join Him in His activity.

This is not just a theological statement; it's a practical experience. Very practical changes are required daily in how we live as individuals and how we function as churches if we're on mission with our Lord, experiencing His powerful presence working through us.

UNRELIEVED PRESSURE

At Faith Baptist, it was this aspect of adjusting our lives to God that provided the most deeply felt moments in our adventure of following God. I would describe this process as the unrelieved pressure of living under the lordship of Jesus Christ as He worked through His body, Faith Baptist Church, to accomplish His will. It was joyful. It was painful. And it was deeply fulfilling.

> *I would describe this process as the unrelieved pressure of living under the lordship of Jesus Christ.*

We had so many adjustments to make to Him as He led us! And because of Him, we had many adjustments to make to one another also.

All our adjustments came as a result of what we came to genuinely believe about who God is, about who we were in Him, and about how He worked in and through us to accomplish His will. The adjustments were necessary because of the truth we came to understand in this passage:

> "For My thoughts are not your thoughts,
> Nor are your ways My ways....
> For as the heavens are higher than the earth,
> So are My ways higher than your ways,
> And My thoughts than your thoughts."
> ISAIAH 55:8–9

Adjustments are required because God's work requires God's ways, and His ways are unfathomably higher than our own.

THE DANGER OF WORLDLINESS

In the Scriptures we see that even when God's people made a covenant to follow Him, they were too quickly influenced by those around them. Relying on the world's thinking and philosophy, the world's gods, and the world's resources soon became a way of life for them.

God warned His people constantly of this critical danger. Even before they entered His "Promised Land," God's warning was clear:

> "You shall make no covenant with them, nor with their gods. They shall not dwell in your land, lest they make you sin against Me. For if you serve their gods, it will surely be a snare to you."
> EXODUS 23:32–33

It's easy for our ways to be dominated and even controlled by the world around us. But Jesus said, "My kingdom is not of this world" (John 18:36), and Paul warned the Colossian church, "Beware lest anyone cheat you through philosophy and empty deceit, according to the tradition of men, according to the basic principles of the world, and not according to Christ" (Colossians 2:8). Kingdom principles are not the world's principles.

Kingdom principles are often seen as paradoxes, and therefore they don't make sense to the world. Several of these paradoxes manifested themselves to us at Faith Baptist, and we struggled with them—as individuals and as a church—until we better understood God's ways.

We learned, for example, that to have any "greatness" in God's kingdom meant that we must be a servant of all (Matthew 20:26–28). We had to "die" to "live" (John 12:24–25; Galatians 2:20). If we tried to save our lives, we would lose them; if we gave our lives away for His sake, we would save them (Matthew 16:25). As we saw that selfishness has no place in the Christian life or the church, God gave us constant opportunities to practice that truth. When we were given opportunities to start a youth ministry or a prison ministry, or to work among North American Natives or among college students, all of these demanded time, finances, patience, and long-suffering. In mercy, God came over us and filled us with His love and enabled us.

Our danger is to trust the world's principles to accomplish our work and neglect the paradoxes of God's principles, especially by failing to trust and rely on His presence and activity in carrying out our mission. But God still says to us today, as He did to Zerubbabel through the prophet Zechariah, "Not by might nor by power, but by My Spirit" (Zechariah 4:6).

THE COST OF ADJUSTMENTS

So many times the adjustments God requires will bring costs that we must bear. In every decision we make to obey God's will—both individually and as a church—we make two decisions. One is what we will do; the other is what we will not do, because we're choosing to do God's will instead. There's a cost involved in both decisions.

I have mentioned some of the costs to my family, as well as to our church, of the mission activity that God led us into at Faith Baptist. Besides our sacrifices in time, finances, and resources, the necessity of prayer became a costly experience for us as well. So much work was being attempted, and we were impelled by God's Spirit to pray. In everything we did, we were in prayer throughout our days and late into our nights. We learned much about spiritual warfare, and many victories were won that could be explained only in terms of prayer. We learned also the cost of spiritual concentration as we "waited before God" extensively.

Such costs are true on the individual level as well. A decision to deepen our personal walk with God—in His Word, in prayer, and in time alone with Him—means the denial of other things. The lonely vigils in intercession deny us sleep. The long hours of ministry to others will deny us time with our families, time in recreation, and time in other pursuits. The discipline of agonizingly searching the Scriptures to clearly have the mind of Christ during critical decisions or to have a word from the Lord for teaching others—all this takes time. And time in His Word cannot be replaced by anything else. There are no shortcuts. The gain is achieved by denial, but the result is worth it.

SACRIFICES

There is always a cost in doing God's will, and I began to see this unfold in very real terms.

We saw a need for someone to live in a distant town where we had started a mission church, and we prayed and asked God to choose someone. A college student and his wife responded. But this would mean much extra cost in travel for them to drive into Saskatoon each day for school, and this couple had so very little.

I said to them, "We cannot let you do this; it will be too hard on you."

There is always a cost in doing God's will.

The couple replied, "Pastor, are you going to deny us the opportunity to sacrifice for our Lord?" I openly wept before God and with them as they counted the cost and said yes to the Lord.

There was hardly a person who did not become involved in sacrifice, because we were doing God's will. A gracious widow, Ivah Bates, who had farmed all her life, responded joyfully to our need for help with a down payment on the building and property for our Prince Albert mission church. She gave two thousand dollars. Her daughter, a former missionary to India, told us later that her mother's total bank account for her support was only a little over four thousand dollars. "But she wanted to give," the daughter told us, "and joyfully believes the Lord will take care of her needs."

I wept again. Several years later I learned that God had not only replaced the gift, but had given Ivah more than she had ever had in reserve. I don't know how this came about, but I do know that God blessed His servant.

CRITICISM AND OPPOSITION

We also experienced the painful cost of having others criticize or counter our efforts. Not everyone understood or agreed with what we were doing, and some actively opposed us at almost every mission church we started.

Though we were totally convinced of the awesome

spiritual darkness around us, some did not see it. In Regina, the capital of our province, a full-page newspaper article appeared condemning us for daring to start a church in this city of 150,000.

In a smaller town where we were planning a Bible study, a delegation of leaders from another evangelical group came to my office, urged me to stop, and assured me that our effort was "of the devil" and that they would oppose it.

Our pastor in Deschambault was cursed on the street by a witch doctor. I received letters condemning our efforts in Prince Albert. And we were told of a meeting in Blaine Lake dedicated to praying that we would fail and withdraw.

Some in our own fellowship of churches said that we were foolish to attempt new mission churches when we were so small in number. We were also told not to come for help if we got into trouble with salary support for mission pastors or other staff workers. Some thought of our efforts as "presuming on God." I soon discovered that any step of faith could be interpreted by others as presumption.

From our study of God's Word, we came to the conviction that no matter how much we might be misunderstood or even opposed, we had no right to do anything but remain faithful to God and to His people. We could not withdraw from fellowship with our sister churches and try to do our own work in isolation. Self-centered independence is not a New Testament pattern.

With other churches, we really are our "brother's keeper."

Later, as our mission efforts grew and flourished and became self-supporting churches, our critics realized that this was indeed of God, and they were encouraged to take similar steps of faith in starting mission work. God helped us remain faithful to Him and gave us a heart full of love toward these fellow believers, knowing that we were doing His will and that He would reveal this to them.

We came to see that in our relationships with other churches, we really were our "brother's keeper." As churches we must be ready to use every means to assist one another in carrying out the assignment God has given each church. The New Testament pattern of the interdependence of churches must be recaptured and lived out before a watching world. Then together, churches will be on mission with God, doing together those things that each cannot do alone. What was said about New Testament Christians will then be spoken about us: that we "turned the world upside down" (Acts 17:6).

In time, God honored our church and our staff, and we became a leader among evangelical churches in

Saskatchewan and in Canada. We helped others start a variety of ministries and to catch a vision for reaching our nation and our world, and our people were chosen for ministry leadership positions throughout Canada.

Chapter 7

OBEYING HIM—
AND SEEING
THE RESULTS

*"Be faithful until death,
and I will give you the crown of life."*
REVELATION 2:10

Regardless of what we say, it's what we do that reveals what we as a church or individual actually believe about God and His will for us.

Biblically, it's impossible to genuinely believe one way and live another. "Faith without works is dead" (James 2:20, 26). "If anyone [or any church] loves Me," Jesus said, "he will keep [practice] My word" (John 14:23). And He asked, "Why do you call Me 'Lord, Lord,' and not do the things which I say?" (Luke 6:46).

It's always in the practice of His will that we are tested. And it's only in the doing of His will that we grow.

For any church, being on mission with God—hearing Him, believing Him, adjusting to Him—requires the cultivation of a thorough disposition of obedience. The Christ who lived His life in complete obedience is fully present in us, and He will enable our obedience. He will not fail to put our lives—individually and collectively—into the middle of His purpose.

Every church can expect God to take the initiative to tell them His assignment; once this is known, there must be an immediate response of obedience, trusting that He who is leading will sustain and enable the church to fulfill their task.

> *"They will be healed, and everything will live wherever the river goes."*

Such a relationship with God means a daily denying of self and a deliberate choosing of His will over our own. It calls for a simple, unchallenged following of the living Christ as He manifests Himself and His will in our daily lives. And we must be committed to helping each other in the same obedient relationships with God.

We can also know with assurance that deep experiences with God will follow immediately upon our steps of obedience. God will see to it. Obedience to God unlocks the experience of His power. It leads to our open-ended usefulness to God and to great blessing and far-reaching encouragement to His people.

A RIVER OF HEALING

One of the most amazing discoveries in our walk with God as a church was how open-ended, full, and never ending were the consequences of following Him. What began as a small act of obedience, issued into a fountain of blessing; our church's thirst for God issued in a flow of "rivers of living water" (John 7:38) as the Holy Spirit worked in and through us in open-ended, ever expanding activity.

Looking back, I can see how our church experienced the picture God gives us in Ezekiel 47. It's the picture of a river flowing "from under the threshold of the temple" (v. 1). The river flows from the throne of God to the ends of the earth. Then God describes its invigorating qualities for "every living thing that moves": "They will be healed, and everything will live wherever the river goes" (v. 9). Along this river's banks "will grow all kinds of trees used for food; their leaves will not wither, and their fruit will not fail. They will bear fruit every month, because their water flows from the sanctuary. Their fruit will be for food, and their leaves for medicine."

V. 12

This nourishment and healing was indeed, in every way, what our church was experiencing. From the throne of God, His mercy and grace and love flowed to us, and then through us, wherever God directed its flow.

SEEING THE RESULTS

The stories are many of how these rivers flowed outwardly to bless a multitude of people. We could never have imagined how far-reaching God's activity would be as a result of our obedience.

For example, our faithful response to God's invitation to pursue a student ministry led to the salvation of many students, among whom were Gerry and Connie Taillon. Gerry and Connie were single when they were saved and baptized in our church, and God later led them to be married.

Gerry soon felt called of God into the ministry and responded to an expressed need to help teach Sunday school on the Cochin Indian Reserve, ninety-five miles away. He faithfully drove the trip each week. Later, the believers there called Gerry to be their pastor, and with his family he shepherded this church while finishing his university education.

He later began a church on Saskatoon's west side, then went to seminary in the United States. After his graduation, our Canadian churches called him to serve in Montreal as our first missionary to French-speaking Canadians. He has been a catalyst for the launching of many French-Canadian churches and the calling out of many Canadian believers who will go across our world to other French-speaking countries. Gerry was later elected by our Canadian churches to guide our entire work across Canada.

Many other stories like that of the Taillons could be told in recognition of God's faithfulness. Not the least of them is what He did in my own family. There were many times, while doing pioneer mission work and raising our children, when Marilynn and I had no resources to meet the challenges confronting us as a family. But God's hand of blessing was extended, and the people of Faith Baptist reached out to us in love and kindness. The effect of this love is still being felt; God has called all five of our children into full-time ministry, and it will not surprise us if He calls our six grandsons and seven granddaughters to serve Him also.

GOD CALLS

God has been stirring His people. His people today have heard Him give this charge: "Go into all the world and preach the gospel to every creature" (Mark 16:15).

Such an assignment seems impossible to achieve, and so it is with men. But with God it is possible—and so the task and calling remain before us, confronting us all. Each person and church must respond.

When Jesus gave the disciples His assignment to go into all the world and make disciples of all nations, He added this promise: "And lo, I am with you always, even to the end of the age" (Matthew 28:20). God's call is not a program, but a Person to be followed, a Person who has given His personal command to be obeyed. And as we obey, He will then accomplish His purposes through us and give every person in our world an opportunity to hear the gospel.

GOD'S PROMISE

God's promise to His people of old is still preeminently true today, in each of our churches:

> If My people who are called by My name will humble themselves, and pray and seek My face, and turn from their wicked ways, then I will hear from heaven, and will forgive their sin and heal their land. Now My eyes will be open and My ears attentive to

prayer made in this place. For now I have chosen and sanctified this house, that My name may be there forever; and My eyes and My heart will be there perpetually. As for you, if you walk before Me…and do according to all that I have commanded you, and if you keep My statutes and My judgments, then I will establish…as I covenanted…."

2 CHRONICLES 7:14–18

May God grant that we shall…
  hear Him…
    believe Him…
      adjust our lives to Him…
        obey Him…
          and fully experience Him in our day!

Multnomah Publishers
The publisher and author would love to hear your comments about this book. *Please contact us at:*
www.lifechangebooks.com

Henry Blackaby Ministries exists to help people experience a life-changing relationship with God that dynamically affects their home, church, and business through a message of revival and spiritual awakening.

We seek to help people experience God through preaching, teaching, conference speaking, leadership training, the production and presentation of ministry materials, and various media outlets including radio and the Internet.

For further information about Henry Blackaby Ministries, please contact us at:

Henry Blackaby Ministries
P.O. Box 161228
Atlanta, GA 30321
hbm@henryblackaby.com
www.henryblackaby.com

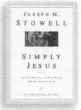